Breaking Free
On the Wings of Forgiveness

Breaking Free
On the Wings of Forgiveness

Erica Felisa Thompson

Stephen Seth Thompson

Erica Felisa Thompson & Stephen Seth Thompson
2017

First Printing: 2017

ISBN 978-1-365-67327-6

Requests for Public Speaking Engagements/Workshops/Study Groups

Please contact Erica & Stephen

Email: Breakfreethewingsofforgiveness@gmail.com

Dedication

To God, without you there would be no us, it is through you that we live, move and have our being.

To our Family, we didn't get to choose each other but we did choose to love each other through the good and the not so good.

To our Pastors, thank you for challenging us to grow in God. We also would like to especially thank you for the vision of the house for it has truly changed our lives.

To our military family, and friends, thank you for always supporting us in everything we do.

Contents

Introduction

The word forgive is often times seen as a choice. "I can choose to forgive or I can choose not to forgive." However, forgiveness is as necessary as it is for us to breathe. It is not just a choice but a necessary action that takes a lot of heart work. When we choose not to forgive others we are only hurting ourselves, keeping ourselves from growing or moving past the moments in our lives that hurt us.

Hurt in essence needs fuel to live. To hurt is to harbor and fixate on pain. This does not mean that pain is avoidable, just that it may start off as a cause and effect and then grow in to something even more. Take a seed for instance. When it is planted into the ground it is still just a seed. It grows when it is watered and nurtured to grow into whatever it is supposed to become.

If the plant is not nurtured it will soon die or wilt away. The phrase, "you reap what you sow," is hardly applied when forgiveness is involved. However, it can if you were really open to examining the situation. Think about it. One hurt, one situation that caused for a forgiving heart, often leads into feelings of insecurity, low self-esteem, emotional bondage, doubt, decreasing faith, depression, anxiety, paranoia, and the list could go on and on. This hurt has now earned the center of your life, the lead character on stage running the show.

Unfortunately, almost every action afterwards, draws from that center. Your choice in friends, significant relationships, your marriage or lack thereof, job choices, how you treat people, how you parent, the level of risk that you're willing to take, can all be affected by that center. This center can even reflect on your sense of self-worth, and does extreme damage to your mental health whether you realize it or not. To go a little deeper, you have walked into idolatry. For the hurt that has so easily beset you have become your focus the driving force that moves you.

In the writing of this book and the consultation of friends it was deemed more important to capture real life situations and teachings from biblical concepts than to write one story. The goal is for readers to be able to turn to chapters that they identified with and focus on those scriptures and solutions from that chapter as a guide for their lives concerning forgiveness. However, I will caution readers to always go to the source no matter how knowledgeable the writer may be on any subject matter. By source I mean God and His written Word. John 1:1 states:

"In the beginning was the Word and the Word was with God and The Word was God."

We are not biblical scholars, just a married couple who are joined together by God. Our titles include woman, man, mom, dad, husband, wife, sister, brother....and the list goes on. Most importantly, though we are believers of Christ who have realized that no matter what the situation, the Word will breathe life into you if you allow it. No weapons formed against you shall prosper, and by weapons we are referencing the unseen weapons of doubt, hate, disgust, guilt, shame, despair, etc. Therefore we are asking you to read on with an open mind. Allow the following stories to shed light on some of the things that may hold you in bondage. After each story unfolds, utilize reflection as a tool for you to journalize your thoughts. Yes, this book is meant for you to write in as your story is still unfolding. When you're done with this book hopefully a paradigm shift will occur; a shifting of the mind that will in turn cause your spirit man to rise up and allow God to mend those broken pieces.

While the reading of this entire book is encouraged if there is a situation that speaks more strongly to your heart and it's an issue that you find yourself struggling with, please do not treat this book as a traditional novel and go on to the next chapter.

Instead, take the time to read that particular chapter over and over again and apply what you've learned to your life. Your feelings form into thoughts, and then to words, which, eventually comes out of your mouth either in the form of spoken word or actions. It is our hope that our words reflect our love for Christ. Psalms 19:14 states:

"Let the words of my mouth and the meditations of my heart be acceptable in your sight, o Lord, my strength, and my Redeemer."

Keep in mind that the act of forgiveness is not as simple as dotting your I's and crossing your T's, but, a necessary, digging deep within "heart work." A mind shift, a change in perspective, and closure will all be necessary in order to move on with your life.

Now this is Erica talking so let me let you in on a little secret....yes, picture me whispering in your ear, it is perfectly okay to "Cry It Out." Cry unto the Lord and cast all your worries and burdens unto Him. Who said that you should hold everything in and carry it all on your shoulders?

When I was younger I remember listening to Erykah Badu singing a certain song. It goes like this "Bag lady, you gon' hurt yo back, dragging all them bags like that...." Think about it, how does the bags of life (includes hurts, disappointments, and worries) benefit you? Every situation, every person that you have chosen not to forgive, is a bag that you have CHOSEN to carry around with you. This choice is stifling your life!

So is this supposed to be a prescription for success? A prescription for living a happy and joyous life? Unfortunately no, because in my opinion that book has already been written. Yes you guessed it. God's written Word! It is with high hopes though, that this book will benefit God's Kingdom. And while there may be other books out there that cover the same subject, hopefully, this reading will spark the change that you would like to see in your life and others around you.

Yes others around you. Did you know that your lack of forgiveness is not only affecting you and your growth, but your loved ones as well? If there is one thing that we'd like you to take away from this reading, it would be to allow for spiritual growth to be your fuel, instead of your past hurts and disappointments which will only take place when you allow God to be your director and liberator. Look to the Hills from which cometh your help and allow your relationship with Him and the Holy Spirit to change your perspective!

Chapter 1: Innocence

I remember being called into the room tempted by

a bag of chips, Cheetos to be exact. Sexually abused by my stepfather... I remember thinking is this what mama goes through? No wonder she works all the time and is hardly ever at home. He promised that if I ever told anyone that he'd take my life. That night I contemplated taking his life, but I thought of my mom and the consequences of my actions. What would happen if I went to jail? Would he then do the same thing to my brothers? It did not help that I was being jumped at the bus stop by most of the kids there. I had to suffer abuse just to go to school only to come home to even more abuse. I laughed at the word love. How can love hurt so badly?

There was a point that I tested out his threat. It was our family game night. I wondered if my mom would really not believe me if I told her, as he so confidently boasted.

Before I could even finish my sentence, a winding blow impacted my face, causing my teeth to bleed with my mom sitting right there. It wasn't the punch that hurt the most, but, the fact that he could do such a thing in front of my mom.

The hurt that I felt when she opened the bathroom door and asked me to repeat what I said was indescribable. I'm almost positive that she heard me the first time. After all, he heard it and he was further away than she was. I knew then that his boasting was not in vain. Convinced that it was a lost cause, I said nothing.

I was 12 years old when I finally told her and my aunt. I remember making my sworn statement and my stepfather going to jail. Deep down though I wasn't surprised when my mom's stance on what happened changed and she started saying things like "I can't live without him" and asking questions like, "what's going to happen to you and your brothers if I can't take care of you?" Eventually she suggested that I needed to re-cant my statement. On one of his calls to my mom, he even promised my brothers that if they kept his secret that he would buy them a Nintendo.

The day that I went to the police to recant my statement, felt like a knife penetrating the very depths of my heart. I felt as if a part of me died that day. What had I done that was so bad that I deserved this life that I lived? I gave birth to true hatred in that split second.

Yet, God presented an angel in the form of a case-worker. She saw beyond the surface and stone like demeanor and asked me to look her in the eye. She proceeded by asking if my recanted statement was true.

Finally a person that could see me and all the hurt that I was going through. Finally a person could hear the voice that wasn't being heard. It was in that moment my walls caved. Crying uncontrollably I told her the reason I had recanted my statement, that my mom loved him more than me and said that she couldn't live without him. She made me a promise and kept true to her word that he would never touch me again and even though I had recanted my statement that I would not have to go back home.

After asking if there was anyone that I knew would take care of me, she called my grandparents and from that day forward my life changed. In hindsight though it took a lot of heart work for my life to change and even then this pain that I carried around for years, always found a way to manifest itself. See it wasn't the abuse of my stepfather that I couldn't take my mind off of.

It was the fact that the one person that should love me the most, chose what she defined as love over her own child. I promised myself that if I ever found myself in love that I would never choose it over anything of importance. My definition of love was faulty. Therefore my love of self was faulty. My sense of self-worth was faulty. I was living in a mind state of faulty perceptions and beliefs. In spite of this, true love shown by grandparents, church family, counseling group, and biblical teachings, became my daily prescriptions. A true paradigm shift didn't take place until these prescriptions penetrated the root of all my issues, a lack

of FORGIVENESS.

****

Reflection

Instead of focusing on the details of Innocence's

story, take a moment to read God's definition of love.

If you read

Corinthians 13:4-7 NIV, love is defined in plain sight

by acknowledging both what love is and what love is

not.

"Love is patient, love is kind. It does not envy, it

does not boast, it is not proud. It does not dishonor

others, it is not self-seeking, it is not easily angered, it

keeps no record of wrongs. Love does not delight in

evil but rejoices with the truth. It always protects, al-

ways trusts, always hopes, always perseveres."

Knowing what's of God and what isn't is paramount. Your definition of love has to be reexamined before true forgiveness can even start to take place. Acknowledgement of what actually happened in the situation is also necessary. Innocence's story is not as uncommon as you might think. Although healing and growth may occur once you are removed from the situation, the issues and problems will still prevail and underline the decisions or lack of decisions you make in the future.

Let's take another look at love as the written Word actually paints a picture for us to examine and live by. John 3:16 states:

"For God so loved the world that He gave his only begotten son so that whosoever believes in him shall not perish but have everlasting life."

His Word also commands us to "love our neighbor as we do ourselves." Unfortunately we as people are not perfect and we get this particular scripture all wrong. When we are commanded to love our neighbor as we do ourselves, it is my interpretation that God is talking about a love that is not faulty and without blemish.

Many times when this is not being carried out as instructed, it is because at the very root, the person responsible for the display of love does not really love his/herself the way that God intended. So, what is love at its core?

We truly believe that God's written word got it right. Love takes work and is an action verb. It is not something that is automatically given but is an action that has no choice but to be reciprocated a hundred times over. The mom of Innocence represents years of engrained insecurities and was most visible in this story. This could very well be a generational curse that presents itself over and over again until the next generation remove this curse at its very root. The mom in this story definition of love was lacking to say the least but if we were to dig deep who knows what misperceptions, doubts, or insecurities would surface.

By no means am I providing an excuse for the mom, only trying to show you what happens when a foundation is built with weak, flimsy, or faulty materials. The same goes for materials that are not faulty but wrong for the job.

When trying to describe this concept to children I always resort to the story The Three Little Pigs. There was a moral to that story. And I believe that this story's moral can be applied to our lives as adults. As you may recall, the first house was built with straw, the second with wood and then the third built with brick. Only one material withstood the blows of that Big Bad

Wolf.

The Bible gives us a story as well. It tells the story of how we should equip ourselves. It tells us to not rely on the traditional body armor but to rely on God. Can you recall the story I'm talking about? The story of David and Goliath. For the person who has not forgiven has chosen to allow his/ her own Goliath to take control over his/her life. That Goliath has taken the form of an unforgiving heart and has turned into negative energy.

"Negative energy can cause a chain reaction in every part of our lives. Be very careful of what you allow into your house- hold. No I'm not talking about the building that for the most part is struc- turally sound. This is in reference to our souls, our mind, our heart."

~Erica Felisa Thompson

Take this time to answer the following questions:

What is your definition of love? What does love look like?

_____

_____

_____

_____

_____

_____

_____

_____

_____

_____

_____

_____

_____

_____

_____

_____

_____

_____

_____

_____

_____

_____

_____

_____

_____

_____

Write down your thoughts on Innocence's story. In what way if any can you relate? What advice would you give Innocence?

_____
_____
_____
_____
_____
_____
_____
_____
_____
_____
_____
_____
_____
_____
_____
_____
_____
_____
_____
_____
_____
_____
_____
_____
_____
_____
_____
_____

Chapter 2: Stranger

I never could understand why you seem to dislike me so much. I mean what did you see when you looked at me? I don't remember spending that much time with you even though I stayed with you for a while on many different occasions. I was the first grandchild but never really felt like it. So what was it? I have no pictures with you almost like it was done on purpose. I don't understand what happened. You tried to take me away from my mother to get a check. I told grandpa once he got home, he was not happy. Had my mother crying at the door cause the people told her she can't see me anymore. Turned out those people were from Child Protective Services. They talked to me although I can't remember what they were saying. I remember thinking "I don't know why they are asking me questions, it's not like I'm at a stranger's house. The next day I heard a knock on the door while I'm playing in the bath. I hear yelling, then my other grandma comes in the bathroom with a towel, took me out of your house, put me in the car and took me home. I think a couple weeks later they came to check on me. At the time I was outside playing, so nanna called me up through the window and said this man had some questions. He started to say things about you and that you had called. He also talked about how my mother left me. He started to discuss taking me with him and making sure I was safe but Nanna made sure that was not an option. My Nanna told him "If you need to check something, check it now," and told me to go back outside and play. I don't remember talk-ing to you or even sitting in a room with you since that incident. When we were in the same room you would give me a look or I would just walk out. I was told you had cancer but I didn't think much of it then. I went to see you before I left for Texas and you were doing ok. Soon after, you were back in the hospital...a couple of months later you were gone. Weeks before you died I was trying to get home just to say I love you. Before you were gone, in spite of all the pain, I loved you. I think I was hoping you felt the same and would say it back but never got the chance. All the days up until your funeral I was fine. My aunt and I drove around talking. I'm glad I was there for her. I thought I would be fine... I just felt different.

So much happened that day and all I felt was numbness. I guess once I got to the casket that all changed. What was cold, buried away, hidden deep inside came flooding out. It was like the tears, the sobbing had no end. I was told I blacked out crying at

your casket. I remember my mother being scared to

touch me and Nanna refusing to. I think part of the

reason I took it so bad is because I waited so long to

change our relationship... So many unanswered ques-

tions...So many tears over a woman I hardly knew. I

carried you around year after year, every Christmas

brought back memories. For me, Christmas was not a

day to be celebrated for it was only your death that I

remembered. The sadness, the hurt, the pain of feeling

unloved, unwanted, rejected.

Reflection

Many times we give people in our lives God like

status. When they fail us (and often times they do) we

cannot for the life of us figure out why. This unknown can oftentimes create distrust, paranoia even.

Another thing to remember is that when someone or something is rejected walls are often built up. This becomes a natural defense mechanism to protect no matter who or what comes our way. Good or bad. We've been rejected so we expect to be rejected. The wound that needs to heal is never healed, only bandaged. Therefore, you are easily wounded again. If feeling rejected, it can be hard to believe that God loves you. He loves every part of you, every flaw, every imperfection, for He is the beginning and the end.

We are here to tell you that you can believe that He loves you my sister/ brother but you must first know Him for yourself. Becoming Intimate with Him is as necessary as the beating of your heart to live.

For the believer that does know Christ as your Lord and Savior, I urge you to go back to your first love, remember when you were first saved? He loved you before you were even born.

Write down your reflections on Stranger's story.

_____
_____
_____
_____
_____
_____
_____
_____
_____
_____
_____
_____
_____
_____
_____
_____
_____
_____
_____
_____
_____
_____
_____
_____
_____
_____

_____

_____

_____

_____

_____

_____

_____

_____

_____

_____

_____

_____

_____

_____

_____

_____

_____

_____

_____

_____

_____

_____

_____

_____

_____

_____

_____

In what ways if any can you identify with Stranger?

Sometimes, when a people feel rejected they turn to what they feel is most comforting. Substances, people, material things, etc. These can represent strangers in your life, or false idols. If it's an addiction it can soon send you spiraling out of control with little will power or self-control. Quite naturally guilt, regret, destruction, chaos, despair, loneliness, depression, shame etc. becomes your companion.

If you or someone you know is currently struggling with an addiction of any kind, know that there is hope. However one must first recognize and acknowledge his/her truth. Then you must ask for God's help and allow Him to order your steps.

Why do we call them strangers? It's because although you are quite familiar with whatever the vice, those vices do not mean you any good. In fact those strangers have many facets and are often underesti-

mated. Chances are even if you think you know the

vice or stranger well, you don't for you cannot effec-

tively see how it is decreasing the value of your quality

of life.

After reading the following poem write down your

thoughts.

Say

No

To

Strangers

Strangers

I don't know why you're hiding

I see you

The one hiding over there in plain sight

You can pretend like you're not there

You and the others

But I see you

You're waiting

What are you waiting for?

Waiting for a time when I'll need you again

See you

Talk to you

I'm not talking, those days are over

Those days of coming back

Falling into old habits

Those days are done

I've changed

The days I had no reason to

But still did anyway

Knowing the difference

Putting on my own blindfold and pushing forward

Trying to justify my ignorance

Lying to myself

Living in a world surrounded by strangers

Allowing those false idols to push and pull me at their
will

Allowing them to consume me

Now I sit here viewing my ignorance through the
hourglass of time

And I see you there like always

Enjoying yourself

Or so you think

The thing about those strangers

Once you shine light on them

There is nowhere to hide

So...... why are you hiding?

I know who you are but time has changed

I'm not submitting to you

Not running from you either

I will not put on that blindfold again.

Instead I'll look to the things above

For I once was blind,

But now,

Thanks be unto God

I can see!

_____

_____

_____

_____

_____

_____

_____

_____

_____

_____

_____

_____

_____

_____

_____

_____

_____

_____

_____

_____

_____

_____

_____

Chapter 3: Wounded

I was wounded by you can't you see? I got saved

under your leadership. I remember like it was just yes-

terday. I was 14 when I gave my life to Christ. I put my

faith in the church and its people. You knew I came

from a drug filled home. That my life was the way it

was due to my mom being on drugs. You knew, but yet

you continued to lead knowing you had a drug of

choice yourself. You encouraged me to help others in

their time of need, why couldn't you help yourself? I

remember seeing your wife try to run you over... I'm

sure she was thinking the same thing. How could you?

You claimed to be a man after God's own heart why?

••

Reflection

Wounded's story speaks of what some call "church hurt." This type of hurt is another form of rejection but quite similar to what Stranger felt.

Why are we most affected by those in the church? It's often the ones that we plant root in, the ones we make a home, that we feel the most rejected by.

Before answering this question we have to understand what family really means. Think about it. The people at your church foster a family environment similar to your family. Now if you came from a dysfunctional family it will be hard for you to discern what family really is (That's another story in and of itself).

In church you have individuals who represent your sisters, brothers, cousins, aunts, uncles, grandparents.... And you develop a relationship with them. You've planted seeds; you've established roots. In essence, you're waiting for your harvest to come, for that "feeling of family." We forget that in a family, people may fail us. This is where the disconnect lies because we forget that our church family are people too. Our blood family can hurt or fail us but eventually we make up. We tend to take on a view of "I may not agree with them but they're still my family." However within the body of Christ, we look at our church family not as people of God but those people become "god" to us, meaning they are placed on a pedestal where they can do no wrong. That's where the rejection, the loss comes from.

God teaches us that all of us are sinners. There is not one of us that is able to cast the first stone. So we have to learn to grow, to mature, and to strengthen each other as a family unit allowing God to grow us up in every area of our lives. We have to stop thinking on a dysfunctional level and think on a Godly level as we grow together in love and by God's grace.

As the body of Christ, we have to learn what family means and what community life represents. We must connect with our brothers and sisters but, refrain from giving them godlike status. We must also keep in mind that God placed us in the body (whatever body He placed us in) as it pleases Him.

Let's go a step further, and talk to those who may have found themselves blaming God, taking on the perspective that maybe God has forsaken them. If this is you, we urge you to read the book of Job, as it can help you in understanding how we are to respond to afflictions/ trials that may come our way. Job's testimony exemplified that just because we are believers does not mean that we won't face hardship. God said that no weapon formed against us shall prosper however He did not say that no weapon would be formed.

Take a moment to write down your answers to the following questions:

What is your definition of family? How would you describe your current family? Your Church family?

_____
_____
_____
_____
_____
_____
_____
_____
_____
_____
_____
_____
_____
_____
_____
_____
_____
_____
_____
_____
_____
_____
_____
_____

Have you ever been hurt by a family member? Your church family? Describe your experience.

_____

_____

_____

_____

_____

_____

_____

_____

_____

_____

_____

_____

_____

_____

_____

_____

_____

_____

_____

_____

_____

_____

_____

_____

_____

What is your definition of friendship? Have you ever

been hurt by a friend? Reflect on that experience.

_____

_____

_____

_____

_____

_____

_____

_____

_____

_____

_____

_____

_____

_____

_____

_____

_____

_____

_____

_____

_____

_____

_____

_____

_____

_____
_____
_____
_____
_____
_____
_____
_____
_____
_____
_____
_____
_____
_____
_____
_____
_____
_____
_____
_____
_____
_____
_____
_____
_____
_____

Think about the top three persons that you consider to be friends. Every heart below represents a friendship. Describe what makes them your friends.

Note: Your definition of both friendship and family will stem from your definition of love and vice versa as love is at the heart of every meaningful relationship. If your experiences are not matching up with your definition take note of this.

No matter how you may feel about your family, your church family, friends, coworkers, neighbors, etc. Know that God sees and hears you. He cares about the very hairs on your head. I pray that you are encouraged by the following poem...

You See Me

Lord, you see me.
You see me for it is evident through your love...
Your love never fails...
It is constant all consuming
Forgiving, merciful, caring,
It accounts for all of me not as the world sees for all
the good all the bad is accounted for
As a loving father Abba you consistently train me up.
It is your love that guides my every step
Making all things work together for my good...
You see me
My inner core
Past the smiles through to my heart for even when the
world may look me over you say that I'm right where
you want me to be, for there is no distraction that can
take your eyes off of me
Yes Lord, you see me
I mean really see me
Through all the mess, all the construction
For even in the molding, the refining, and the sharp-
ening of iron...

You see me
For it was you who created me.
It's your love that continues to be consistently com-
manding me to go forward, to stay on course, on the
path that you have set before me, until your return.
For you never fail, you never quit
You see all things out until it's complete...
For my completion is in you.
May I remain steadfast and unmovable, a reflection of
what you pour into me day after day,
May I Abide in you always, never afraid
Because you see me
You hear me
You know and meet my every need.
It was your love and grace that created me and it is
your love that will create a finish work in me.
For you see me Lord
All of me...
Every breath
Every heartbeat
For it is in you
That I live,
Move, and
Have my
Being.

Our pastors taught us to write down our prayers.

What is your prayer?

Chapter 4: Esteem

Most people's addictions are quite typical of to-

day's society but very few will admit the addiction that

I'm about to share. See, I had an addiction to Esteem,

no not esteem of self but the esteem from others. I was

moved by what people thought of me. Tended to react

accordingly even to the point of hurting relationships.

Not willingly, but I quickly learned that I couldn't

please everyone no matter how hard I tried. I could

give you a sad sob story that focused on the negatives

but I won't because, the good outweighed the bad. I

was raised by a mom who loved me and no I didn't

have much money, but, we had the necessities of life,

the things that mattered most. I wasn't in a bad spot

financially, and no, I didn't have kids out of wedlock. I

had a wife, a stable career, a foundation in God. I thought we had a marriage rooted in Him, but it turns out we didn't. Two people unequally yoked. Looking back on what we had, I think the ending would still be the same, in spite of that heart wrenching day. Two kids who got married way too young, and founded on lust instead of love, friendship and God's Word.

Every relationship that has died had a turning point. That turning point can be the death of the very thing that you worked so hard for. Mine just so happened to involve the very person that I thought I'd never hurt in a million years.

For a time, I replayed that moment over and over in my head. Can you imagine hurting the one thing you loved most in the world? It doesn't matter to me that it was an accident. I'm Dad. I'm supposed to protect. Love showed me just how fragile it was. The life of a human being, a little child, with my eyes, my nose, my blood running through those little veins, my firstborn, let down by a simple act that we had performed countless times before. I'd throw him up in the air, he'd laugh and squeal with delight, then I'd catch him and he'd look up to me from the safety of my arms.

Not on that day though. Not in that moment. Watching other dads do that exact same thing is a constant reminder of that day. That split second where the chain of events took another path. See that day ended differently. I threw him up in the air, he squealed with delight, only to become frightened. I couldn't catch him. He didn't end up safely in my arms. It was in that instant that all of our lives changed. Blood, looked like pints and pints of blood poured out of his nose. My wife and the director of the daycare ran in to see what happened. We couldn't make it to the emergency room fast enough. The triage nurse treated it like a typical nose bleed and had us wait in the waiting room. Still the bleeding didn't stop. I'm not sure if I noticed the swelling then, but I knew in my heart that something wasn't right. I knew that it wasn't a typical nose bleed. I couldn't bear to wait in that waiting room another moment so I told the mother of my child, my wife to trust me and follow my lead. We ended up leaving that hospital after two hours of waiting and going to a children's hospital. It was there that my concerns and fears were validated. My, son's MRI depicted a cracked skull.

So many questions, so much disappointment, such a sight to see. Eyes almost swollen shut waiting to see what would happen...Waiting for the doctor to come in and give us an encouraging report. Waiting for the child protective service investigator to show up. A nightmare except in no way was I asleep. That day was the beginning of our end.

. . . .
Reflection

Forgiving others is much, much easier than forgiving yourself. However, forgiveness of self is imperative! It is a process that you must complete for each time you consider yourself failing at anything you will resort back to those moments in which you've "failed" before. It's almost as if you've created a never ending saga with the main theme being "I'm not good enough." Optimism becomes a foreigner and pessimism becomes your best friend. Self-sabotage becomes your weapon of choice causing everything else to be inflicted with the poison of self-hate.

You may be asking, how do I break this gloomy cloud that's over my life? Know who you are In God's Kingdom! Don't you know that you were created after His own image and made for such a time as this? Seek God in your trial, ask for direction and then wait to hear His voice. And when the waiting seems unbearable, and your future seems uncertain, make up your mind to walk by faith and not by sight!

Can you identify with Esteem's story or know of someone who does?

What is something you have yet to forgive yourself for?

Take a moment and journal your thoughts and feelings concerning the questions above on the following pages.

Do you recognize self-sabotaging behaviors in your

own life? What are they?

_____

_____

_____

_____

_____

_____

_____

_____

_____

_____

_____

_____

_____

_____

_____

_____

_____

_____

_____

_____

_____

_____

_____

_____

_____

Think about this. We control what we hold onto. That need to control could be why we're holding onto the hurt in the first place dependent upon the situation. Many try to control everything and everyone else around them but forget "self-control." Those fruits of the spirit will carry you further and help you to stand even when things look unsure or unstable. Your lens can't be faulty before cleaning someone else's lens. In the same way your lens if faulty/ cloudy can damage another's lens. Blurred vision, fear, lack of self-control, or panic can lead to lost lives....your life or the life of another. What are you anchored to? What are you standing on? If you were a boiling pot what would seep out when the temperature rises?

Many rely on their own strengths but forget their limitations. It is at that point, during testing and trials, which reveals what we are standing on, where we dwell. Where you dwell matters! Even if you fall, your dwelling place, if higher than you, will allow you to get back up.

Remember David? We discussed him earlier. David by no means was perfect. He strayed off course, but he knew not to drown. He knew to repent, to go back to his first love. He returned back to God, for his limitations were far too great to rely on self and live. He did not wallow in self-pity, nor did he give up hope. He accepted his consequences and asked for forgiveness. In asking for forgiveness from God, he also had to release the situation to Him, letting go in complete surrender.

Word of God Speak

It's me again

Down on my knees cause I failed you once again.

I started to hesitate and not ask for forgiveness

Felt unworthy,

But I'm here.

Bowing down at my altar letting it all go.

You said no turning back,

It's nothing to look for back there.

See Egypt is not your home your home is with me.

You pulled me from those dark places

When I didn't know what to do

Stretched out your arms

You said come home

My son you have something to live for

The sins of my parents are not the sins of this son.

The devil was celebrating

Thinking the victory bell was rung.

I received the power from Gods only son

With you in my corner, Jesus

I know my battle is already won.

For you are the chief cornerstone.

Nothing the devil can throw at me

Can stop me from pressing towards the mark

I can feel your presence God

It's time for my soul man to take a seat

And let the spirit reign

Like it was always meant to be,

Word of God Speak.

Chapter 5: Confusion

I feel responsible like I should have did some-

thing. Why did you choose to leave? I miss you. It's

been a long time and it seems like just yesterday we

were playing ball and laughing at everyone. You had

such a big heart and never let anyone change you. You

were my brother, we talked about everything and

would crack jokes for hours. I remember the day you

said you were not going to take your insulin anymore.

I guess I didn't really understand what was going to

happen. We just went on day to day like nothing ever

changed. Like it was never said. You appeared to be

the same as time went on I guess I never saw it com-

ing. I didn't think about it until the day that you were

finally gone. I didn't think about just how important

insulin was to your health. The decision that you were making when you stopped taking your medicine.

I remember the day you died. It started off like a normal day. We went to separate schools but that didn't stop us from walking together. We walked all the way down the hill parting ways, at the train stop. You got on the train, and I walked to the bus stop a couple of blocks away. Two friends on their way to school. It was a regular day. Nothing out of the ordinary. On the way home I started to hear rumors about what had happened. That someone had died on the train. Not thinking anything of it, I walked home, dropped my bags off. I carried about my day not knowing that I would find out that the friend that I considered a brother was long gone. When I went to another friend's house I started to hear rumors that it was you...that you fell between the train tracks due to a diabetic coma. Other friends started coming to the door spreading the same rumor.... I thought it was all a dream...that they were playing some sick cruel joke. Then the phone rang. It was your mom saying it really was you. I remember crying but still refusing to believe that you were gone.

My friend and I decided to go to your house but before we got there the block was full of people writing on the floor in front of your building. Lighting candles saying rest in peace to you. When we finally entered your house all I could hear was crying from your mother and sister.

I remember asking how you could be gone so fast. On our walk back home I started to think. To wonder if there was something I was missing. What was different? Was this just your day to go? I lit a candle for you in the middle of the Court where we used to hang. Cried for a long time just thinking of you not being here anymore but I know you are always with us. Did you fully comprehend that by not taking your insulin you were choosing death....I didn't.

****

Reflection

God's word warns us that the devil comes to steal, kill and destroy. God has purpose for each and every one of us. As His children we must trust Him in every area of our lives remembering that we must seek first the Kingdom of God. Our lives are not our own but are His.

Oftentimes we forget that a person's decisions, actions, or inactions, can be a form of self-harm. Reflecting on Confusion's story, hindsight can be your worst enemy. Hindsight can cause you to put pieces of the puzzle together that weren't necessarily clear as the puzzle pieces were being handed out. While there are signs of suicide or self-harm, a person taking their life is not your fault.

If you are or know of someone contemplating ending their life please reach out and ask for help. Don't allow your situation, thoughts, or emotions to take over. None of us can truly live going by what we think feel and will for that is our flesh rising to control us, not our spirit man. Jesus said in Gethsemane that the spirit is indeed willing but the flesh is weak.

To the disabled, the one with infirmities, please know that you are loved. God loves you just as much as the son/ daughter without infirmities. Remember Johnathan's son? I imagine that he thought his condition was the end of his story that it would prevent him from experiencing a fulfilling life. What he soon found out is that his disability did not define his worth. God's

grace and mercy was experienced by Mephibosheth.

According to 2 Samuel 9:13 Mephibosheth dwelt

in Jerusalem: "for he did eat continually at the king's

table; and was lame on both his feet."

If God were to ask you "am I worth it? What

would you say?

Please reflect on the following poetic piece...and jour-

nal your thoughts based on its application to your life.

Am I Worth It?

When you count up all the costs am I worth it?

The service, the commitment,

The heartaches of life

Am I worth it?

Will you choose to take up thy cross and follow me?

Am I enough?

My life given for yours

My blood for the sins of this world?

Am I worth it?

When weapons are formed against you

When people turn their backs on you...

Lied on like Joseph (have you forgotten that he was

remembered and favored)

Unloved like Leah, (I loved her enough to open her

womb...she was seen and heard...her praise was from

realizing that her connection to me was all she need-

ed.)

Small like David (It was his belief, his faith, his obedi-

ence, his worship and praise that allowed him to be

the one that remained standing)

Don't you see?

When you place everything in perspective...

Am I worth it?

Will you persevere?

Will you endure until the end?

Will you grow past you?

Will you?

Grow...

Past...

You?

Ephesians 4:15 is more than for a season

It's a requirement, as necessary as the air that you

breath, as imperative as your next heartbeat.

I told you that no weapons formed against you shall

prosper...

Will you trust me?

Oh ye of little faith

Why does the wilderness continuously sweep you

away?

Are you that fickle?

Don't you feel the breath of life?

Blown into your nostrils?

Born again...but you still choose death?

Why? Those idols...have become your center...

Meanwhile I wait for you at the center...

To be your top priority.

To seek my face daily, to make me Lord

To choose me, for I won't force you...

Don't you know how much I love you?

I am the way the truth and the life

To be lukewarm, doubleminded just won't do...

You decide, am I worth it?

I kept you from death in more ways than one. I shield-

ed you, held your hand, carried you, and interceded on

your behalf...

Don't you see my hand over your life?

Would you be where you are without me?

What would you say if it were you in Gethsemane?

Is my grace sufficient enough for thee?

I loved you through everything, never left your side,

Called you to myself several times,

I heard your cries...

To quit,

To give up now,

Would be suicide...

So while you count up the costs my brother...

While you evaluate your life my sister...

When you finally open your eyes...

When your ears are fully awakened....

When you become sick and tired of being sick and

tired...

I'll be here

Waiting on you

To make up your mind

To open your heart

To die to self

To bow down

To commit

To receive my word

Finally....

So that you may live

To count it all joy...

Giving your final answer

Once and for all...

Am I worth it?

I guess my name speaks for itself. An island, desolate, and destitute. You left me here alone with a child to carry while I wait. To wait on you my serviceman for a year only to find out that you are the shell of the person I once knew; I feel the numbing of my heart. It's an honor to serve your country. I mean, I'm sure of this fact but it doesn't take away the emptiness, the loneliness that I feel.

You abandoned me. You've changed, no longer my knight in shining armor. While you were gone, I would wait on your phone calls like a person awaiting a kidney transplant. To your friends in the background, laughing, joking around... Didn't quite paint the picture of a person eager to come home. Yet you claimed you missed me. The weeks between phone calls and the brevity of time we did spend talking on the phone said otherwise. I'm committed but this is starting to feel like a death sentence. I've placed my life on hold for your career. It seems to be the cloud that hovers above our heads.

To top it all off you haven't even picked up on the change in me. You pretend that things couldn't be better. Like we are growing closer when instead we are drifting apart. Sure we are together again but at what cost and in what state? There's distance between us and I'm not sure that we can close the gap.

****

Reflection

Our feelings and our thoughts go hand in hand. When we dwell on a particular thought, the feelings associated with that thought clouds our judgement. We come to place where we only see what we want to see. Reading this you may ask how Island wants to see her marriage as desolate. Well although she may not on the surface, her thoughts and feelings have become her reflection. It is what she sees when she looks into the mirror, at her husband, and her life. It's the picture that she has painted for herself. The thoughts and words that she has repeated to herself is like poison to her spirit. Proverbs 18:21 reminds us that

"Death and life are in the power of the tongue and they that love it shall eat the fruit thereof." The word also says in Proverbs 27:19 "as in water face reflects face, so a man's heart reveals the man."

Remember that God is the cord that links you both together. Ecclesiastes 4:12 assures us that "if one prevail against him, two shall withstand him; and a threefold cord is not quickly broken."

What labels have you put on your marriage? Have you given your issues to God asking first for restoration of your sight, your love, your commitment? Instead of looking outward take a moment to look within. God sees and cares about you. What would you like to say to God about your marriage, household, and your children (if any)?

Chapter 7: Helpless

I always felt like I failed you because I wasn't

there. I thought you were safe, but was always nervous

because I knew how the streets really are. I always felt

responsible.

I never thought I would get that call. My mother told

me you were gone, that it was three days since anyone

had seen you. I feared you would be gone forever. My

mind went from fear to anger as mom continued

talking. Why did it take so long for anyone to call me?

I was slowly processing what I needed to do then I

realized that I was too far to do anything. How did I let

this happen? If I was there, I would have been with

you. I thought I prepared you for everything. The next

few days I wondered what you were going through. My

thoughts soon went to the worst...were you still alive? I called and called trying to get information trying to see what was going on.

Then a couple of days later I received the news that they found you. However the place they found you just made my mind wonder... I could only imagine all the pain that you had to endure. The cops found you and called the house. When they arrived they had the pamphlet of prostitution saying you were captured, forced to sell your body for someone else's pleasure. I cried for a few days after the news. I didn't know what to say to you so we talked. I tried to see what you were feeling, how you were doing, what was going on with you? You never really talked about it.

I don't think I really wanted to know the details because the thoughts in my mind were hard and painful enough to know what you really went through.

I felt like I was there at the same time you were. Captured alive, wondering for days when you were going to get found, if you were ever going to be found.

You weren't even that far from home. It must have been fear that kept you there. It felt like the light you had in you was taken away and replaced with nothing but darkness. You were never the same after that, pretending to be happy when I know all you felt was pain. I blamed myself for years because of what you went through. I should have been there to protect you.

****

Reflection

When we feel responsible for what happens to someone, especially someone we love, guilt is often the companion to a negative event. It's important in many situations to look at what's actually within your control. Even if there is a situation in which we are to blame, we have to get to a point where we can move forward instead of reliving the negative event.

One problem lies within our attempt to "make things right again." We can't fix a person because we are not saviors, God is. A person that has been hurt needs a listening ear not sympathy or pity for that matter. Strength is gained through intercession, through our prayers. In addition, seeking guidance from the One that can make them whole, the One who gives us a peace beyond our understanding, is imperative.

Jesus said in Mathew 11:28 KJV

"Come unto me, all ye that labor and are heavy laden,

and I will give you rest."

Another problem lies in the feeling of helplessness itself. At least when you don't have the revelation that when you decrease on purpose God can increase in your life exponentially. This is very different from feelings of hopelessness and self-defeat.

We as humans will never have all the answers. However, we know of the One who does. It is up to us to go to Him, to call on the comforter, the Holy Spirit in our time of need.

What are your thoughts on Helpless' story? Have you ever felt responsible for something bad that happened to someone?

Chapter 8: Imprisoned

Looking back I wonder how things would be different if you were here. What kind of father you would be? I think about how some things might have been different, a lot easier. So many unanswered questions. Would I have had a regular childhood? I don't know. For most of my life I have seen you locked up, and it was hard. Everyone use to say I was just like you in attitude. Was I really just looking in the mirror? I felt a lot of self-defeat. As a child I needed you. It was so much going on and I had to grow up fast. It was difficult but I had to adapt to the life I was given, even if I felt like it was unfair. I had faith that you and I would walk the streets one day. Silly right? Not sure that will ever happen.

As I got older I started to feel as though I was destined to fail; that I would lose my life or be in a cell next to you. Over time I got used to holding my emotions in, never letting anyone know how I was feeling. When I would visit it didn't really feel like father and son. I could never truly vent to you, never tell you how I felt. It didn't matter though, because I would go through the same routine. Seeing you time after time with no real connection. It was more for you than for me. I'd leave with a little hope, only to realize I was going back to my own prison.

With the passing of time, life became more complex. Truth be told I started to dislike you. You loved to take pictures but no matter how many pictures were taken, the fact was that you were not there. I had to walk this walk alone. Imprisoned... I had my own cell that I had to live in. The only difference is mine went with me everywhere I'd go.

I remember the day you were released after over 20 years of being in prison. When I saw you, I felt like that child all over again. I was overcome by a tidal wave of thoughts and emotions. So many memories, so much hurt but for once in my life I felt as if I had someone to lean on.

We talked for the next year and a half and then you decided your freedom didn't amount to anything or your family either I guess. Maybe all this time, prison was your home. We didn't matter, I didn't matter. But yet, you want me to write. Why should I write you letters, what do you want me to say?

I think the hardest thing is being in a relationship with God knowing that the Word says honor your mother and your father. I mean how can I? I have children of my own. How do I tell them that their grandfather has been locked up for most of my life? I can't go back down that road. I remember feeling so small, so lost, so distanced from reality filled with the fantasy of actually having you around. No more time for fantasies I have a family to take care of. I stumble enough as a father not having an example of my own. Why should I uncover old wounds?

****

Reflection

They say save the best for last. Well we saved Imprisoned's story for it is a story of a dad who has a relationship with God but has difficulty following and adhering to God's commands. It appears that he's reached that one area in which he is hesitant to let God in. God may be calling him deeper but Imprisoned has chosen to remain close to the shore.

In what ways can you relate to Imprisoned? Write

your thoughts down on the following pages.

Keep in mind that everyone has to make their own choices in life. The dad in this story has had to live his life and continuously have found himself behind bars. It is the only life that he knows. But Imprisoned knows of a different life. Each day that he goes to that alter without forgiving his father he's rejecting God, for God has placed His word in Imprisoned's heart.

What do you need to give to God? What Word has God placed on your heart? Please take a moment to answer these question on the following pages.

It is imperative to really look at what Imprisoned is. Imprisoned is not just representative of a place, it's a state of mind. It causes you to not place trust in anyone or any situation. It stunts your growth and leaves you lonely; always cautious, waiting for something bad to happen. The walls that are built up, may protect but, they also block God from getting to you. You can't hear when your ears are clogged. You can't see when your vision is blurred. Ultimately the way is through forgiveness just as Jesus gave his life for us and forgave our sins.

In John 14:6 Jesus said, "I am the way, the truth, and the life. No one comes to the Father except through Me."

Some may ask, what does my relationship with God have to do with forgiveness? We don't have all the answers but we challenge you to consider the following. That situation, that person, that negative event, is over and done with. Sure there are remnants of it, meaning that you were obviously affected by what happened. However, you are still STANDING. Why are you choosing to allow whatever happened to have power over you? For those that proclaim that it doesn't, what motivates your actions/inaction? Where does your anxiety, fear, depression, distrust, guarded behavior, etc. stem from?

If you can trace a lack of forgiveness at the root then it is definitely time to forgive.

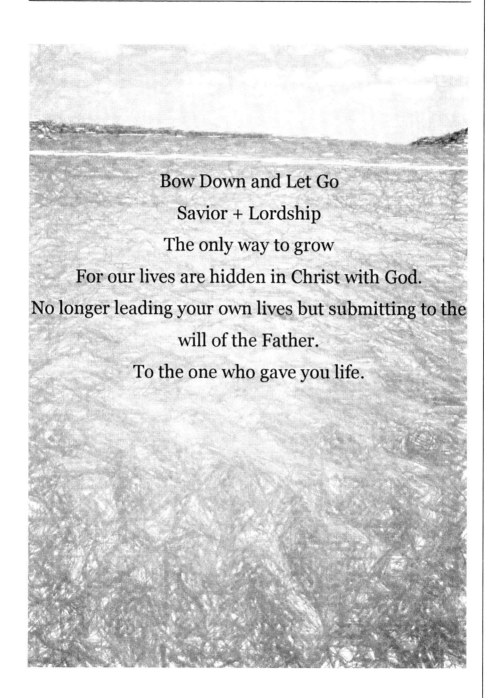

Bow Down and Let Go

Savior + Lordship

The only way to grow

For our lives are hidden in Christ with God.

No longer leading your own lives but submitting to the

will of the Father.

To the one who gave you life.

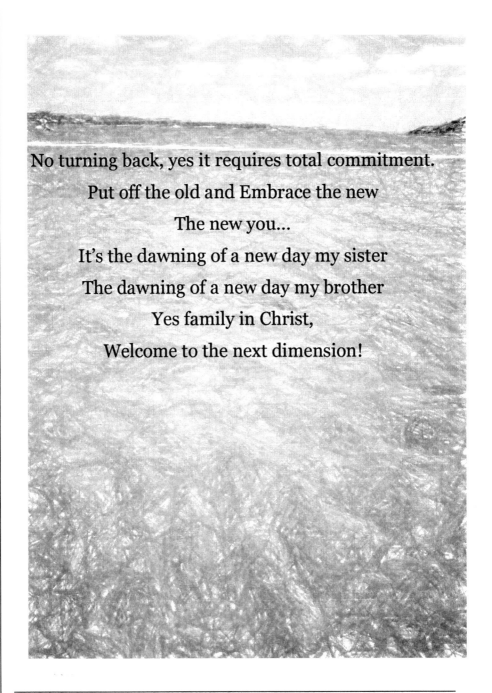

No turning back, yes it requires total commitment.

Put off the old and Embrace the new

The new you...

It's the dawning of a new day my sister

The dawning of a new day my brother

Yes family in Christ,

Welcome to the next dimension!

I Erica Felisa Thompson am Innocence. I share this information to show you that your VALLEY is a TES-Timony in the making! Your PRESENT will become your PAST so don't allow current circumstances to determine your FUTURE.

I won't sit here and tell you that forgiveness is easy but it is easier than allowing a lack of forgiveness to shape the rest of your life. Looking back I realize that God kept me. He gave me strength to endure, hope to believe, and faith to see past my circumstances. Most importantly, He reminded me who I am and that my identity lies in Him. He loved me when I didn't even love myself. And just when I'd start to believe those intent to harm me, He gave me vision, purpose, and a deeper understanding of who He is. He healed a broken heart, gave discernment when I struggled with trust, taught me to challenge my fears, lay all my burdens at His feet, and to forgive. He gave me light in the darkest of times and compassion when hatred and anger wanted to take over. He protected me and assured me that no one or nothing could ever take my joy.

****

God has been stripping and washing away, molding and shaping us. We've learned of the importance of growing up into Him in all things.

Our pastors have reminded us to remember our first love. To be intimate with Him to put Him first, and with

Him we'd have it all...to include family. God gave us family outside of our biological family. It was amongst family that we learned to come to not just the house of God but the God of the House. It's where we've learned to be fitly joined together, to be accountable, to know that everything works together for our good.

We've also learned the importance of writing our own prayers and vision for our lives, and that continuous Growth in God is paramount! Maturation in God is a lifelong process.

Mathew 5: 3-12 in the message bible is a scripture that helps us in our day to day. This scripture reminds us that we are blessed. Therefore, we pray that this personalized word of God is a blessing to your lives as it is to us.

Remember that you are blessed even in the wilderness!

I am Blessed

I am blessed when I'm at the end of my rope. With less
of me there is more room for you and your rule.
I'm blessed when I feel I've lost what is most dear to
me. Only then can I be embraced by the One most
dear.

I'm blessed when I'm content with just who I am-no
more, no less. For in that moment I've become a proud
owner of everything that can't be bought.
I'm blessed when I've worked up a good appetite for
you God. For God you are food and drink in the best
meal I'll ever eat.

I'm blessed when I care. At the moment of being 'care-full,' I find myself cared for. "I'm blessed when I get my inside world—my mind and heart—put right. Then I can see God in the outside world.

I'm blessed when I can show people how to cooperate instead of compete or fight. That's when I discover who I really am, and my place in God's family.

I'm blessed when my commitment to God provokes persecution. The persecution drives me even deeper into God's kingdom.

I am blessed for with you Jesus I have everything.

Yes love, you are blessed! Therefore, set it in your heart and mind to forgive. Give it to God and ask for His divine help. Then join us in...

Breaking Free

On the

Wings of

Forgiveness!

CPSIA information can be obtained
at www.ICGtesting.com
Printed in the USA
LVOW12s0328020218
565034LV00003B/221/P

9 781365 673276